Titanic Ideals,(Think Outside the Job & your Employer's Box)

TABLE OF CONTENTS

Title Page……………………………………………I

Copyright……………………………………………ii

Table of Content……………………………………iii

Acknowledgement…………………………………..v

Dedication…………………………………………..VI

 Introduction……………………………………vii

TITANIC IDEAS:

'THINK

OUT-SIDE

THE JOB

&

YOUR EMPLOYER'S BOX'

DISCIPLE ERAGA E. JACOB

DISCLAIMER:

The author and publisher of this book specifically renounced and disclaimed any liability that is directly or indirectly incurred from the use of the contents of this book. This publication is solely designed to provide much-competed information concerning the subject matter covered by this book. The author and publisher are not also engaged in giving legal advice. If legal advice is required, the service of a professional should be seeked: info.jeafservices@gmail.com

ACKNOWLEDGMENT:

I Acknowledge Nigeria Youth for this work. They inspired me into the written of this book because they are hard working people.

DEDICATION

I dedicate this book to my children: Abraham.

Isaac & Eraga Jacob Jnr

COPYRIGHTS

All Rights Reserved. No part of this publication should be republished, store in a retrieval system, transmitted in any form or by any means – electronic, mechanical, photocopy, recording, or at others; except for brief quotations in printing reviews with prior permission of the publisher.

Titanic Ideals,(Think Outside the Job & your Employer's Box)

CONTENTS

INTRODUCTION: 11

CHAPTER ONE

IGNORANCE KILLS FASTER IN ALL THINGS............... 14

CHAPTER TWO

ACTUATING IN TODAY'S WORLD BUSINESSES........... 18

CHAPTER THREE

THE RICH BUYS YOUR TIME AND KNOWLEDGE........ 26

CHAPTER FOUR

TEST HOW YOU THINK IN THE 38

MIDST OF UNSEEN OPPORTUNITIES.......... 38

CHAPTER FIVE

KINDS OF BUSINESSES 49

CHAPTER SIX

JOB SECURITY VERSUS FREEDOM.......................... 64

CHAPTER SEVEN

ERAGA JACOB'S VIEWS ABOUT GROWING FROM MALL......85

CHAPTER EIGHT

A PROCESS PROSPER A VISION………………….....93

CHAPTER NINE

BASIC THREE FORCES FOR GROWING

RICHER IN BUSINESS……………………………….122

CHAPTER TEN

HANDLE YOUR DEFINING MOMENTS……………...132

CHAPTER ELEVEN

WHAT IT TAKES TO BE GREAT……………………...136

CHAPTER TWELVE

DO AWAY WITH DARKNESS (CORRUPTION/EVIL.....145

CHAPTER THIRTEEN

ZERO BASE SUCCESS………………..151

CHAPTER FOURTEEN

THE VERY TITANIC STORY-YOU WILL LEARN 187

INTRODUCTION

This book is written to address the problems, <u>poverty</u> ,and <u>unemployment</u> in most part of the world.

The book *<u>unveiled the bottleneck</u>* faced by employers, employees & the unemployed in the working industry, and teaches how <u>to escape</u> the slavery in most cubicle jobs and its associated poverty.

The Book will help us <u>become</u> the kind of good persons we *may have chosen to be on our jobs, and on the work on our hands* and how to become a <u>creative and independent thinker</u> with <u>*the ability to think broad*</u> and <u>*forge ahead*</u> when there is no responsible government & lucrative jobs that may take care of our financial needs today and in the future.

In the instance of no jobs to do at all, and in a state of miserable and reduced earnings, with this book, you should able to know what to do. The book taught entrepreneurship, introduces businesses mix, positive attitude development &

recovery of interest from entanglement and depression <u>even when the</u> economy meltdown.

This Book also uncovered the *Basic three things you need* to grow your <u>desired business peak into success successfully</u> for a significant financial dominion. <u>mail: info.jeafservices@gmail.com</u>

CHAPTER ONE

IGNORANCE KILLS FASTER IN ALL THINGS:

If we want to know a person more, play golf game with him or her. The golf game is a mirror that views a person's true core value and business behavior pattern. This purpose is the befitting secret behind the game of golf that thousands of people do not know.

Often, when I want to know who I am about to do business with, I will play golf game with the person. As we are playing, I am not much concerned with the score as I am with how he/ she play the game- By "Why We Want You to Be Rich, Two Men. One Message"

Be careful about whom we have in our working team. First, play a game of golf with them because most workers and advisors do not have the experience we pay them for in the service they provide us. They advise us to turn our money over to them for investments into businesses which they hardly put their money into. They convince us to believe they know it all and are experts with the eagle s' eyes in the market places. When the market crashes, you will get to know that they do not know it all.

Majority of the financial advisers often market or sell the food they do not eat. Most marketers also call the financial advisors, or salespersons do not invest in what they advised others to invest their money into. Many investors/entrepreneurs fall a victim because they thought it is every financial advisor that has insight, foresight, and hindsight of the market places.

When we refused to know what we do not know and solely rely on people's knowledge, we may wreck our initial capital through financial advisors or team. A financial adviser will think for you for a paycheck. Are you the kind of person that thinks all financial advisers knows the market well? It is not always so when it comes to business. Learn the best that is supposed to know in your business. Self-ignorance in business kills faster in business. When the initial capital lost, it is forever. Knowledge gives us the big money we may be looking for per time.

CHAPTER TWO

ACTUATING IN TODAY'S WORLD BUSINESSES

Mediocrity must be in zero tolerance for sustainability in this era of globalization in commerce and industry. Commerce is the lifeblood of the whole world. The person or nation at the peak of this industry controls everything.

Business today aim at world class services delivery. World class status business is one that meets peoples' need through supply of better products, cheaper, and faster and retain them.

Business is today about sensitivity to a need and processes. First class Status in business is practicing excellent service.

The characteristics of world-class enterprises is a drive of customer satisfaction which is the ability to meet needs in the merged global economy, attitude development, organizational processes, and strategies to develop superior customer relationship, and exceeding customers' expectation with higher quality service with lower cost, faster delivery schedules, and safety.

Entrepreneur attitude development is first to succeed in the globalized economy of today.

Processes are cross-functional sections/units of an enterprise. World class enterprises sustain itself as the best in its field with a full range of those services from the beginning to the end with regular follow-ups in meeting customer need for their retention – This should be our drive in business.

World class status enterprise is a knowledge base leading company. This knowledge is a composition of a refined attitude, quality information, experiences, training, and talents. Knowledge is the most suitable in this global economic phase.

Knowledge in business management is providing the right information to the processes at the right time in business. Knowledge base management aligns different categories of information including customer wants which helps an enterprise to compete readily.

Knowledge of business also takes the form of ideas, learning, understanding, memory, insight, technical skills, capabilities and capacity in work. Knowledge is the asset an enterprise use to grow. This is the value of stakeholders that keep and maintain competitive advantages of an enterprise.

The corporate process is a cross-functional operation as a milestone toward achieving world-class status in business.

To achieve customer satisfaction goal, we must have the right people in the organization with the right attitude towards work, have the appropriate job process defined, so that we would ensure consistency of plans, execution processes, information safety, decisions, actions, measurement of result for a good reward.

Knowledge is a must to attain world-class status in business. World class status in business is when we make business a deal better. In this case, an enterprise undergoes realignment and periodic processes assessment to determine corrections and do changes necessary to be done.

This assessment is a review which examines the quality and scope of each process, programs, services, and determines how efficiently they meet the enterprise objectives and each process contribution. Knowledge is the working capital that is needed in businesses.

Assessment of the processes and key performance index helps to align individual or a team contribution to the company with the overall goals of the entire enterprise or company.

Business review is also critical; it provides the impetus for further planning to effect appropriate changes systematically as change is inevitable.

World class status in business is base on wisdom, logistics, and techniques. We must know the best concerning a business.

World class service Solution Company is a company that thrives for excellent service delivery. It begins from reception and front desk, customer service table who decorated the customer for retention to survive in this single competitive global market. With this enlargement, it is undoubtedly only knowledge base functionaries in the industry that will undoubtedly survived in the commerce and service industry.

CHAPTER THREE

THE RICH BUYS YOUR TIME AND KNOWLEDGE

Making business ideas a success requires financial intelligence, skills, and instinct. It all depends on knowledge.

The big challenge and threat in our economy today is poverty of temporary/ contract jobs. Most of those contract jobs are not suitable. The second big challenge is pension Funds scheme in which the employee and employer pool a certain amount of income together into saves to when the employee is laid off or retired. The pool cannot take care of them for life.

The third challenge is the higher and fire brigade approach of sacking the junior and top senior workers in the working industry because the companies cannot pay their salaries again to curtail cost or meet their new desire change. Majority of those people are sack without proper retirement benefit plan for them. The financial intelligence for wealth procreation among job holders and the unemployed is therefore necessary even when the rich buy their time and knowledge temporally or forever for this undue cause.

I do not want people to be swallowed in by financial challenge when they leave the job or in the absence of no job to do. We are in the era when employers make it know to the employees they were not going to take care of them in the future or when they retired.

If we are employees without good take-home pay, how much have we saved as a pension planner that will take care of us? This pension plan on which the employee and the employer contribute a certain percentage of their income into one pool as retirement settlement is naïve and a symptom of dryness and hopelessness. There is no truly a plan for the employees' future here.

Having a business is like growing a tree for that our unpredictable future. As the tree keeps growing, it is expression of a glorious future because it augment your paycheck and secure our future.

We should be prudent.

Have a quality financial control in spending money and have a business that is representing you. If something represents us, we would want it to be the best representative of us mostly when it is an issue of having financial freedom.

The job we are holding that is not giving us reasonable money may not be our good representative. No one retains what does not glorify him. This practice is also one of the reasons many are financially crippled and begging for money.

Many people get jobs to be able to pay for the immediate things they want. Some do the jobs they are doing because the jobs have trapped them, while some are just to survive. To retain that job without financial options is an impoverished setting and poor permanent mindset to live to just live to survive hunger.

Even some of the financial advisors live permanently in hunger due to poor financial intelligence. You need knowledge to change bad financial situation. What I am telling us here is how we can change our financial situation not necessarily our job mostly when the job makes us small, hungry, and smaller than a person we are. This is when the job is holding us and making us to live a life of lack and want (mediocrity).

Many people left schools only to be traped/ caged in jobs that make no meaning and fulfilment. Awareness is the first step to a new thing and progress. I am giving it here be in focus.

Where we are and what we do is determined when it comes to the matter of wealth creation because it influences our cash inflow for economic liberty.

Many people are just trapped financially, waiting to earn more but not knowing what to do. It is easy to do what financially successful people do if the knowledge is there. It is also easy to have the result of financially successful people. I am revealing this secret because I want us to have financial freedom, and not to beg anybody to take care of us because we may not get a satisfactory help or get it in the first place.

Have a vision and know all that is supposed to be known in the business representing you.

While holding the job, also use the spare time well. Those who are ready to gain freedom work extra hours.

Let me reveal this secret: The employer has bought your time and the knowledge. That is your total pay package or a take home. No one eats his or her cake and have it back. Time and knowledge are what they bought from you. They ensure their time paid for is well utilized on the job. Some employers have because of this time issue seen a staff career development as nonsense while on their job.

Many staff left their jobs for school due to the time problem inner conflict between them and employers.

The only advice some employers give is that the job should be hold very tight; there are no jobs, work! Work! Work! They will never advise you to augment your income by doing other part-time businesses because they are scared. They are scared because doing another business with the time they have bought already makes no sense to them. They may also be scared of the possibility of diverting the resources you are entrusted.

Let me help us do a little thinking here. Though the employee will undoubtedly lay off one day; the impact on the company never dies where our joint efforts have in no small way built.

The earlier a worker begins to use the brain faster the better. Become an entrepreneur. I cannot think for you more than this. We may say "we do not have enough money to start." I will introduce us to some businesses to do with broad knowledge and with small money in this book. Be a creative thinker first.

A business is an art know it. A business is an act, do it. Nothing is wrong in doing a genuine business with the spare time you have while holding the job that is not feeding you well. We can grow that small business into *The Very Titanic- Titanic Idea.*

Employers should not be selfish to teach their employees how to create wealth to be financially stable than to still depend on people for money while holding a paycheck job with them. Teach them how to strategize not to be financially handicap and crippled when they live the job.

CHAPTER FOUR

TEST HOW YOU THINK IN THE MIDST OF UNSEEN OPPORTUNITIES

We can <u>respect something</u> without having to <u>embrace it,</u> but when it comes to financial freedom, I recommend both.

Financial breakthrough is not a day something. It is grown as ideas and experience that were developed in many years ago. Something can take centuries to evolve.

There is no one formula into financial success in the school of wealth procreation. But almost every financial success hangs on discovery and idea crafting.

Life is about changing what we do not like. I do not think much of a man who is not wiser today than he was yesterday and today. Every day has a better way. How I did it might not necessarily work for others, but we watch successful tracks and how the rich think and had gotten it done. We may copy from them and embrace their steps. This is a formula that has worked for some people, not necessarily only me not me.

See the following image I have; we can embrace it as a formula for wealth procreation. You can hack and craft it:

What is this image?

<u>Your views please</u>:

<u>my views:</u>

(a) _____

wooden image

(b) _____ (b)

human head

(c) _____ (c)

Pictures of a person

(d) _____ (d)

money?

Whatever are our individuals' views, I would like to tell us another right side of it we may not have mentioned. The difference between many people is that they can be seeing a golden idea anywhere they are about a particular thing. Millions of people can give different name and meaning to one thing. Some people are constructive and creative.

My Real View: Creative thinking is the new order of earning and spending money.

Many dreams how they should suddenly build and dwell in empire, and forgot how to build it in the midst of uncertainty.

What I see in the above picture is money. When you shall sell the above-carved image from the tree in the forest at your backyard, you will get the universal currency-dollar.

We kill a spider that spread web (poverty) with knowledge. This is how to stop poverty that causes crisis and crime (web).

I saw dollars not a wooden image at all. This is how creativity procreates wealth. I am not a Rich Man that is secretive and pretends he does not like money. I educate others on how to build fortune/ wealth so that they do not beg people for money.

All the economy trees in the bush of Africans are dollars. We become rich when we are creative and acted promptly. We are poor because of the way we think. I cannot think with peoples' brain for them, but I can guide them and open their eyes for viewing properly. We can make it anywhere we are. We becomes what we think and do.

We create time to read, and know much about what we chose doing. For instance, reading this book is a good starting point. When I wanted to write this book, 'titanic ideas' to be successful in it, I sat down and planed what I should say and how to write it down to run the reader.

What I see is leverage which is the ability to do greater things with less or no opportunities. We become how we think and see.

There are opportunities where ever we are. With a vision, there is no better place than where we are.

I have combined my talents with the job am doing, using logistics methods studying the work and the environment for the leverage I see no one else may see. Someone can only be poor in a rich environment when he or she does not see leverage. A person can be rich in a weak and dry environment when he sees leverage. When we see no opportunities but stress and weaknesses we are calling poverty. This is the reason we may be poor.

Sit up. Leverage is seeing opportunities where others see only weaknesses. People who are determined to live above poverty are careless about discomfort in their environment. Knowledge is our leverage and everyday has a new money to give us.

We are above the situation we are complaining. See that challenge as an opportunity to doing great things. There is always an opportunity. It might be closer than we see it.

The land is here, the man power is here, the knowledge is there, the small money is there to make the big money we need. We have traveled large and far and have seen great agricultural exploits in places like Indian, Israel etc. Why are we crying of poverty? It is because of laziness, greed and corruption. These are the sacrifices we must give out to experience all round peace.

'We kill a **spider**

that spread **web**

with **knowledge**'

CHAPTER FIVE

KINDS OF BUSINESSES

(1). **Real Estate Business Management:** This business involves land properties management. Some buy lands, builds, and developed land and houses to flip it. Moreover, some own houses for commercial purposes not to flip them. This business is good because Banks can finance it while paying back through rent charges, retention fees, and through house furniture allowances paid by tenants.

The hard thing in this business is on how to have landed property, uncompleted landed property or work in progress to buy and add value to it and make money with it by flipping it when it has appreciate.

You need knowledge of real estate business in the area of Land Use Act / Ordinance and Regulations Control on lands usage.

The Zoning Ordinance / Regulations control how we use our landed property. It is a law that guides cities, townships, state governments, local government and individuals on real Estate or Agricultural Development to shape the community.

Land Use Act prohibits specific developments in certain areas. Some lands are zoned or apotioned for commercial buildings only, Agriculture, Industrialization and so forth. If we fail to find out what uses are allowed as estate developer in your first step, it can be an expensive mistake when it turns out Law Use Act prohibits your development.

It is a good idea to hire a Local Land use attorney to help review the land use plans and the options for handling land use concerns. Zoning / Land Use plan changing is not easy to come by. It is difficult to change the land use plan already done by the government because of a single individual.

Under the land use act in Nigeria, corruption in the process persists and has made the cost of obtaining C of O (Certificate of Occupancy) high and even not obtainable on application and request in five years by the none politically exposed persons in Africa(Nigeria). Unlike in the past, someone could buy a piece of land and register it at the Land Registry ministries once.

Once a land is registered, it becomes a bankable asset with the document (C of O). This has stopped many nigerians access to loan and it hinders development. If you know much in the business of Real Estate Management you may financially prosper.

(2).

Entrepreneur: This is a person who set a ball rolling. He is an owner of a business call a product.

He is a discoverer, an inventor of a product, a thinker and the first user and marketer of the product. He launches it.

What this business requires to blossom are instinct, ideas, foresight, insight, hindsight, and hard work.

Entrepreneurship is what makes people survive economic crush.

Entrepreneurs are people who like to try something new every day and a new way of doing it.

Entrepreneurs are those who feel they own the world something and give it out to it. An entrepreneur discovers what is missing or sees a problem and provides its solution. There are always problems, find one and provides the answer

As M.Twain has said, don't go around saying the world owes us a living. The world owes us nothing. "It was here first". The world was here before we came in. It owes us nothing.

We own the world something, give it out, and we go back. If we want to go far in life, and when we want to be fulfilled, we find or create a problem to address, and then give the solution. That is the spirit and happiness of an entrepreneur

(3).

Trading: This is a form of business that requires the spreading of knowledge and working capital into business opportunities in the form of buying and selling for quick returns. Here people buy your knowledge on line and pay you. If we are into this form of business mostly now the world has become a tiny global place through technology, high financial cost and other expenses are reduced.

We earn money here and pay no tax at all or less.

We can be general Merchandise with this setting or business outfit and making progress and grow Big as business owners.

The knowledge we need most in trading business is to know figures and how to read and write. Then we watch where people want to meet immediate need and we do it. That is all.

In trading, working capital floats. Savings is not necessary for trading business because turn –over rate determines our earnings. In saving money at the bank, the investor takes a big purse into the bank and small purse out of the bank. A trader/merchant takes big steps in and bigger steps out. This is the difference between a depositor/saver and a portfolio diversifier

(4).**BIG Business Owners:** They have business software and process that do almost the whole work on automation. They lead in their businesses, few employees do the control with him, and many do the work.

Business owners have free time and buy others time and make much money through them. This is part of their success.

(5).

Self Employed Person: This kind of person does all the work to see it done right. They do not build a business as the entrepreneur. He works very hard and with much time. They see themselves as hardworking and keep the secret of the work from others; but are full of stress and likely to have ill health, low cash flows even though they took all the profits.

(6).

An Employee: This is a person working for another person. They may not go to school at all. Some go to school to get a certificate with a low or high grade and get a safe or unsafe job at times or many years. He does the work for a fixed salary and pursuing a standard pension plan with the employer to when he or she is layoff. These are the group of people the employer buys their time and knowledge basically for their work. If the time is not there or knowledge of the work is not okay, they call it a day.

It is naive and dangerous to only hold up to a job that does not provide us with the money that meets our needs and establish us.

(7). Investment in Stocks and Bonds- There are two kinds of investors: passive/ Defensive investors and Active or Enterprising Investors. Every business requires a sound intellectual framework about the business. The result we have sometimes depended on the efforts and intellect applied in the business concern.

Stocks and Bonds are paper assets. Essential elements involved in specific choices in stocks are Historical patterns of financial markets over many decades, knowledge of how the various types of bonds and stocks have behaved under varying conditions

The underlying principles of sound investment are inside business information, knowledge and attitude. Knowledge is number one because it helps to avoid serious mistakes or losses that will sink the business.(8). Digital /E-Commerce Entrepreneurship: This is on line or electronics transactions developer. This includes learning how to develop webs, blogs, software developments etc.

CHAPTER SIX

JOB SECURITY VERSUS FREEDOM

Let us face the real business now.

Focusing is important. Some people have failed because of what they have heard, thought and believe. Refuse to join failing group.

That failing group probably does not belong to us. At school, I was told that getting a good job after my school is the way to fulfilment and indeed to love, and lives in happiness and peace; mostly living in financial dominion.

I was not told it leads to uncertainty and a complete lack of control over my life. Life is time. This assumes that an essential aspect of that life God has given us is controlled by other people mostly when we do not see and feel to have achieved fulfilment on a particular job. It is scary for many to start their own business but just start and you will grow.

We struggled to get the job, and we still struggle for our job security. We have freedom when we are an entrepreneur or business owners. Those two things are not the same thing at all- holding only to a job and owning work. Holding a job means being placed on payment while owning a work make us pay for other people's time and knowledge. This makes us employers of labor.

Those two things have opposite values. People holding jobs are facing jobs and financial insecurity, bad health and have the least freedom.

The most important things we need to be at this excellent state call meeting financial needs is time, knowledge and little money to make big money.

When we are holding a job for a payout check, we work to secure our job by using our time and our knowledge for the pay check.

What our employer pay us for are only two things: our time and our knowledge for the work. These are the two things we are paying for. Knowledge is the asset an enterprise use to grow because it drafts the company's vision and mission (direction and controls)

Many jobs holders are not also allowed to express their creativity and innovation while on the jobs.

They are not in control. Henceforth, I see you as a mechanical designer, a draft person with the goal of firing his boss to be boss or own a business.

Employees do things based on the instructions given to them. They are afraid not to lose the jobs. They answer sir, (oga) when things are either wrong or right.

To them, conformity is not or never a dull moment. Instead, they preach their employers' message and do what they are told to do.

Discretion will be missing, and potentials are inferior and also underutilized on the job.

Your employer is the one in full control. It is the time and knowledge they pay for, gaining by using the time and knowledge of yours for the work given to you . That is why people are hired. The 10 percent who take the 90 percent of the cash benefits/ profits of the company does not do the work that the 90 percent of the other people (job holders) who does the work earns. Sometimes someone can be doing something foolish and of less or no value without knowing. None sense.

Many employers are no longer offering a flexible range of benefits for compressed work weeks and weekend jobs. They now recruit those who are happy to plod along till retirement. You are not that person.

Employees are also fired when the salary or take home pay is now making the company to be operating at loses as he grows higher on the job or when it is discovered that there are cheap labors somewhere with lesser charges with better input and output.

Employees may not necessarily be fired because they do not know the job or have done a wrong thing, but it can also be as a result of new changes to be enforced in the company where you are holding a job. This is why we say jobs are not secured. Someone may be fired.

Employee's exits do not flag problems for some companies again. Before, high staff turnover was a threat to be investigated andaddressed in a company but today, staff exit is initiated by the employer. Many companies do not even conduct an exit interview to seek the reason for leaving voluntarily from their jobs.

Changes are necessary in an organization every day, but it takes place slowly. The company holding a job with may take a new management decision to accelerate its desire change. Those changes at work are usually ungrained culture to unlearn to learn new skills and methods. New hands may necessarily be employed to change old ones on the work mostly when the desired goal of the company can be sabotaged and sees unattainable when that old staff is still on the job/work.

The employees' years in the service might no longer be in a long range to profit the company on their new long-range plan also, so there will be the need to fire the old employees for a new intake. Today, employers are as interested in staff working life balance with the necessary training and the paycheck.

The change can be a structured approach to minimize disruption and cost. This happens to ensure the desired profits and benefits plans are achieved.

Today many employers are no longer given their employees a sense of self-sufficiency while Workers are increasingly flexible and adaptable meaning that they no longer continue working for the same company for as long as the employer needs them. A change also sees these threats, obstacles and eliminates them for ease enforcement of the desired change.

The company may change its processes to automation and technology where much profit is made with little or no human efforts.

Those changes affect the psychology and emotions of both employers and employees (the inner fight between employer and employee). They are risks and opportunities for both employees and employers. These are some of the risks on the job not formally defined in detail of the distinct parts of the job which affects how employee behave from day to day while on the job.

I once trained staff for my own business and placed them on salaries. I saw them before I closed my eyes, but when I opened my eyes, I saw them no more due to a change management.

Fine!

It is because management change might have affected them. Employee's interest can never be higher than the interest of the whole organization when it comes to a change. This psychological aspect defined what happens to your paycheck and the job in the present and future.

This book is helping you to expand your right thinking and to be financially intelligent. Invest the earnings, be creative and innovative.

Our retirement benefit is not also well planned by our employers to take care of us in old age when retired.

Brothers help each other not to suffer by saving each other through straight talk. I recommended that we take advantage of the above discomfort of hire and fire's tragedy on jobs to have a business. Be an Entrepreneur or a business owner.

We can all benefit from each other through the power of right thinking. To be intelligent is a big plus for everyone. Intelligence is the ability to solve problems. I want to help us to solve a problem live. In life, if we can solve problems, we are considered to be intelligent. When it comes to the school of financial management, the more prominent business problems we can solve using our instinct in business is financial intelligence, and the better the prospects. Government Officers and jobs holders should have reasonable business intelligence quota.

Today our world faces severe financial handicap, problems like hunger, unemployment as a result of poor or low business and financial management knowledge and support as a result of:

- Corruptions

- Indiscipline

- Low Financial Literacy

- Unfairness/ Dishonesty

- Greed

- Lack of sound commercial usage policy etc.

The reason a kind of my person speak out is to educate us because we want people to become aware and at least to be able to solve their little financial problems rather than expecting others to solve their whole financial problems for them when they are old, displaced or at the instance of no job to do/ when they are layoff.

What most companies owners teach their employees is that they should live below their means so that they can save, take care of their health via the health insurance scheme, to save for their children's education through particular insurance scheme plan, etc. The question is this, what will we do since the retirement plan, and insurance will not take care of us long? Can the cheque take care of us as soon as we leave the job? All our savings and the stories 0f live below means would not be able to take care of us and our family members that are not working also due to the unemployment problem.

We do not have control over that job but today we can when we are at liberty in the spirit of entrepreneurship. Today I am in control because nobody wears me in and off as bangles on the wrist of a woman. I am in full control of what I do now, and I have liberty. "That is what I do sir."

Our governments can no longer pay salaries regularly; they are now going on a contract job which is a sign of financial roadblock. The problem in our country today is that it runs out of money. Where is the crude oil money for the past four decades? Our past governments were corrupt and have failed us. Nothing is on the ground to reckon on. We cannot raise our stamina in this competitive world of today. Where is the voice of our country (Nigeria) in the world?

One of the reasons I wrote this book is because I saw what you had not seen. I saw those things in practice. I do not want you to be a victim of them because they are still there and they are still coming and going around. I am not trying to be a person that is not positive. I want us to know the truth and aware of what is on ground, hoping to put some of us who are willing to know on the right track before it is late. I am in the position because of my personal experience and drive to the success and a fulfilled kind of person I desire in my life. I am doing what Superior people do. I address the societal problem- corruption/ evil, building values with understanding and knowledge so that we may be free from evil, poverty and crimes.

CHAPTER SEVEN

ERAGA JACOB'S VIEWS ABOUT GROWING BIG FROM THE SMALL

We invest only two BIG things and one tiny thing to be rich: (1) Time (2) knowledge and (3) Small money.

The rich get richer because they buy others time and knowledge and pay them tiny money. The big money comes from time and knowledge. What someone does with time matters. What employees own their employers is time and knowledge.

I chose to increase means by working harder with my spare time and knowledge. If we sleep four to five hours a day after closing from office, then what do we do with the remaining time?

If we refused to learn, if we refused to use the brain well, many will end up getting and living on job with paychecks that do not give financial freedom.

A great book I read recently is, *Why We Want You to Be Rich* written by two different minds: Robert Kiyosaki & Donald Trump. They were both businessmen. I recommended this book to anyone who wants to grow big financially.

Knowledge is the money and power to do exploit. Learn to be an expert and do things alone. Most of the financial advisers we have are not as experts as we may think. Most of them want to get richer by giving investment advice that cannot even work well in business. Perhaps most of them are not as expert as we may think, so get the knowledge.

With the power of the brain, creativity, and innovation, someone can move from 'to survive job' to a fulfilling BIG business.

As I mentioned before, many wealthy people are secretive. "I did not realize how much so until my rich brother asked me to quit is family business, which later turns out to my favor and good"

Many rich people do not want others to be known, and they do not want to share their knowledge with the poor. This is one of the reasons the gap between the rich, poor and middle class is getting wider every day and night.

I am a volunteer ever ready to share willingly. It takes much soul-searching to impact others.

Knowledge is a spirit; it exists to impact others positively. If the effect and impact of our lives are to be felt, it does not matter whether a person does not have teeth. This is the reason I am writing us this book just to impact others..

While it is essential to learn from people like me, it is also essential to find your secret formula too.

You should find the formula and method that is working best for you. The way I get it done must not be the way you might get it right. Ok?

Set a goal, find a process, get your secret formula and we inevitably become prosperous persons/nation we desire to be. As an instance, when I was planning to write this book, planning to make it cheap and readable, to mitigate business flaws, it took me time, a style and a process. The same thing we should do in seeking financial freedom. To be free from lack and want is a drive and a dream that is planned, plan yours.

Every dream has a process. Every dream has a goal. Every process is a planed step, and every goal is a result to be achieved. In another way round, a dream is a thought, a process to get something achieved. Go for it.

Think of a dream, dream it. Do it.

A dream has a purpose, and every purposeful dream has a process and its reward. Have a dream, and lives it with knowledge and time.

With the power of the brain, time,

creativity and innovation,

Titanic Ideals,(Think Outside the Job & your Employer's Box)

we can move from just

to survive job into a BIG

business for the big money of our choice

CHAPTER EIGHT

A PROCESS PROSPER A VISION

A Process is as essential as a dream or a goal to accomplished. The process is more important in a dream for the goal to be accomplished. A process of getting something done is critical.

Many are weak because they lack a process. Some are weaker because they lack a vision and a process. Things are done anyhow in a place where there is no vision and a process. There can be no progress at where process and vision are missing. I am advising us to have a vision and a process in anything we do. If what I say is lie, we kindly show ourselves the result we have.

This page is about a vision and finding a process to the vision. It is a process that makes vision a real dream to pursue; it keeps it safe and from misguided idea.

A process is a compass wind; it involves learning how to do something in an ordering manner, to be guided against unprotected conscience not to be taken unaware by distractions. Being ready for something is a process that guarantees victory. Victory is a factorial that takes a process.

What does this mean? We either fold our hands or clap for other nations that are making it in life to be written off, or we study how people win by themselves to be winning and benefit from the ongoing changing trend in the world every day.

Britain has a process; the USA has it, India and China do. This Economics globalization would not favor a country that refused to eschew corruption and adopt a process.

The next general World Economy recession coming up will be hard to escape by countries that do not have a vision or having it without a process.

This intellectual property is for us as a solution tool for our problems solving in Nigeria / Africa and for the underdeveloped world.

This book is not for *'get rich'* mindset. If the intention is to get rich, it is much easier to find free money in oil Region of my state zone: Niger Delta, than this soul-searching work of writing.

It takes a person of integrity, principles, discipline, and commitment to do this kind of work. Sitting and writing a life transforming book is a bold decision that involves making meaning and passing it out to the whole world. It takes pain, separation and a tough time to write. If we would instead join people to make a significant change, a process and decision to change is necessary. Then read on, this book is for you. If not, this may not be the ideal book for you. We take old habit away for a new habit to be formed. This takes a process.

Many parts of the world lack a process. That hinders growth and development. A process is vital for achieving a goal or a dream.

The message is clear here; with a good process we can build our nation high and ride on horses, become more prosperous and peaceful than getting more miserable day by day due to lack of process.

We can be rich quicker by solving our problems than adding to the economic and political problem (corruption). It is a matter of leadership and followership, creativity and ability, solving practical problems with *common sense*.

We spend money anyhow (carelessly) because we lack a process. I follow a process. This is what I do as this reduces my fear and fuels my courage to say and do more.

I think of how our efforts can make our desire to change a reality since we both need a better change.

What is essential is just missing in many people's lives in our continent. What is it? It is the courage to design and embrace transparency and accountability process.

Once we get this right attitude, our large nation will become a better place to live and visit like the USA and most places we are not recognized because of attitude problem.

One of the reasons many people are running away from home (Nigeria) is because of poverty. Nigeria has lived on its past successes, but now, it pushes challenges forward rather than to solve them. Nigeria should come together to fight the siege called corruption. It should not be as only Mr. B or Mr. E agenda. I believe I am saying in other words, that common sense required here is togetherness which a simple plus and minus arithmetic: $2 = 1+1 = 2-0 = 3-1 = 4-2 = 5-3 = 2 +1-1 = 2$ can solve in due process.

Nigeria is a kind of place where people may profoundly celebrate mediocrity, looters, and thieves. Don't you know it is because those perpetrators are underutilized they become the nation's devil workshop?

Whenever I travel to some parts of the country what I see are beggars in the streets, begging and crying for money and food as in most homes of orphans. Businesses are dead everywhere, and I saw many shops and companies folded up, foods are short, and families are hurt in more ways as it has never been. This needed a process. When the government of this nation will be on my shoulder, I will solve those problems.

'Addressing the societal problem corruption & creating values in Africa' is a book written explicitly by this author to address the bad attitude most people put up in the use of money and corruption in Africa. It talked about a change of attitude. It is possible to change everything when there is a change of attitude. That thing we must drop is our bad attitude due to corruption.

I believed the best way to change the rules of the game in Africa today is to change the way we think. Knowledge of truth is necessary for the hygiene we need in our politics and economy. If we have good knowledge, we have had the power to effect the change we all need.

Remember that all we are looking for is progress and peace to be rich as a nation. Go from hearing to doing. Action speaks louder than words.

The thinking process seems to be lacking a lot in many people including some leaders. I do not power crazy, and I am not looking for popularity, but I want to see a change. It is not fun to write. It is annoying and depressing too because someone has to seek nature and stay alone many times to be able to write a book. You must deprive of yourself a little freedom of movement because separation is necessary to write a life transforming book.

With this work in your hands, I feel highly accomplished, very successful and fulfilled because I know with its contents we will undoubtedly change as its guarantees us a success.

We choose the kind of good life to live for ourselves. We either take it or we leave it. When I meet people who live with bad attitude and ways which I know I would not, I feel very bad; I talk to them. I am talking to us here. Please let us come together and do something about our poor state in Nigeria/ Africa.

If the whole world should rise, Africa must rise, and Nigeria should first rise.

I am saying corruption should be trash in Nigeria/Africa. I have not only told us to stop it. We are enjoined to confess and profess fighting corruption in Africa together.

We know corruption is in everywhere, but it becomes a threat and heart blowing when it is a lifestyle of people. This is what I have seen among us.

At foremost, it is a daily discipline it needs, hard work, actions, and integrity if one is to be found fit to fight corruption; but when this is missing, what we see is silence. I may have the advantage of doing this work because I am one of those people who does not require a lot from people. I follow a process in the things I do. So what can stop me from writing a book addressing this societal mess (poverty) and creating values?

Once again, also find the book: Addressing the Societal Problem, corruption and creating Values and read it. It will help us as leaders or followers to have a vision and process, to be impactful and accomplished. I catch up with daily world events and address them as necessary as part of my calling.

Let us quickly see the Nigeria job creation N-power Social initiative Programme here. This Jobs creation and employment initiative social investment programme of the Nigeria Government is a very good one, but it may be deceptive and un impactful if it is not well handled. Anything that is not managed well cannot be reliable, and it does not transform when it lacks a process; and whatever it is that lacks process will ever lack conformity.

N-Power may not just end up as a social initiated programme designed to encourage the youth into creativity, meaning to create jobs, bring entrepreneurial spirit among the youth and for poverty alleviation but also as a tool for economic growth and development if when handled.

It is a good mission initially drafted to create jobs and to encourage the youth into creativity, entrepreneurship, and productivity but it would not last if it is not for the youth skills development and financial empowerment for productivity. It may end in becoming a political strategy to the ascension of prominent political offices, meaning using N-Power platform to encourage youths to cast votes. It becomes a paper house on a rock/ or mountaintop. Anything can happen to that kind of house.

Jobs are created by creating new jobs not by filling vacant positions and making youth apprentices to the existing state government workers/ employees in the various state government ministries.

Many of those N - Power workers even have no jobs to do because the jobs were not genuinely created on expansion formula or the platform of creating new ministries and industries – N-Power is a good vision, but a good vision can become a bad one when it is wrongly driven and lack a genuine process.

A nation without a whole drive and a process can be fighting corruption and still encourage it because they did not fight it.

Today training in our schools is changing. Many technical schools, polytechnics, and Universities now have business schools for those interested in building their businesses. We do not have practical lessons to learn in the business study at schools, but we learn much in practice. Class Paperwork is not the same thing as in practice. Until they practice it outside the class room else, the education/ training will not mean much.

The youth are disturbed and having sleepless nights waiting for the government jobs they have not seen. I think this is the problem the N- Power is meant to address- creativity, jobs creations, self-development / entrepreneurship.

I am writing to address this concern here. It is not only about the youth; also a concern is the country general layoff problem. *Do not wait for our leaders to do it alone, but person to person.*

Our government is telling us lies about unavailable jobs and their jobs creation for the youth.

The government is worse off than what the government is telling us today. With the resources we have, our country is still very bright if honest people who are concerned to make great of our country are giving leadership positions.

If the youth do not stop expecting the government to do everything for them too, we will continue to have the same results. We become a nation filled with well-educated people looking for jobs, free meal; and financially needy. Giving youth the checks to eat today and suffer tomorrow will not solve the problem. Instead, teach them how to do something through creativity and innovation. This will help us out of this mess we put ourselves.

N- Power programme may temporally push forward the problem of unemployment among the youth if not well handled. The truth is that jobs are not created. This is the truth, but these jobs assumed to have been created are too vulnerable. How is somebody without teaching training at school employed to teach at school? 'If you hire an ignorant to teach your child, your child will come out with f9 and later turn out to a thug, only story tellers, and folded hands.

Albert Einstein defined insanity as "doing the same thing over and over again and expecting different results." In this case, it is my opinion that it is insanity to pay youth salaries without jobs / sending them to workshop for business and skills acquisition. Our schools do not teach them how to create wealth and use money (commercial usage Literacy), so we have a horrible commercial usage lifestyle.

Many gifted youths will never be recognized because they have not be developed. Deceiving our youth with free salaries for not doing any work or being trained on how to create wealth is enormous darkness. There are over one billion minerals that are untapped in them. Develop their skills and make them see life beyond sitting idle in the offices and cubicles.

We want them to be creative, rather than expect a handout from the government. That is how we can help to solve the problem of unemployment.

This book cannot help everyone, but it can help those who genuinely have the desire to experience a turn around with creative knowledge. Creative thinking is conceptual and constructive reasoning that helps to bring and keep an idea on a track.

This is also productive thinking. This process is also missing. We need a process.

We must be careful about the kind of teaching, the education we give or receive. Many people want the government or people to always do it for them. I think the major things the government owns us is free education, security of life and property, human development, provision of water and light, and healthcare. The government does not own you your Vision and willingness to act. These are two fundamental things you must have to succeed in life.

The youth should have a vision, and our leaders should dream pleasant dreams.

Mrs. Kim goal is for all women to increase their financial IQ and not depend on men to take care of them. I would recommend her book (a Rich woman by Kim, Robert's wife) for both men and women in Nigeria, Africa, and others so that we can develop the spirit of artistry in us.

If we as a nation attempt to solve the unemployment problem, social security and healthcare and primarily, poverty by giving people more money free, free houses, payouts, the golden goose will be cooked and eaten, that there will be no more golden eggs. It is a deception in the apex. Let us do the right things to save our country by genuinely creating the kind of environment and works by encouraging innovation and creativity for self-reliance among the youth.

My message is clear,

with zero tolerance

on financial and none

financial corruption

we can build our nation

high and ride on horses,

become richer and peaceful

than getting poorer day by day;

we can be a good help to others.

CHAPTER NINE

BASIC THREE FORCES FOR GROWING RICHER IN BUSINESS

I like being straight when I write or teach and encourages others to be rich in the knowledge necessary to excel in their endeavor.

Basic three things are required to be successful and to take charge in any venture. Those factorials are: Time, knowledge and small capital

(a). Time: Time is our life reader. Time is life. This is what employers buy from workers. The relationship between employer and employee is hanged on time. When it is not readily available for the purpose it is needed for, no relationship may exist.

Most people do not see time as life, so they spend it anyhow. Value time or life; Prosperity answers to time. No matter what the struggle, no matter what are the climate factors, time counts most and determines result. We invest time in business than money. Time makes the money than capital. Time is money.

(b).Small Capital: This is the third principal actor in the world. It is planted, watered and grown to be able to answer all things. With enough time, small money is committed to growing big BUSINESS, while broad knowledge keeps the business and makes the big new money.

We start from the very small to the Titanic. We become big from the very small.

Many people do not want to be poor. They do not want to live badly but they are punished by their thoughts about starting small, time, knowledge and money matter.

This book is not good for those who see money as the basic thing require for doing business successfully. We need big knowledge and small money to make big money. It all depends on our approach to it.

(c). Significant Knowledge: This is discernment, foresight, hindsight and intrinsic value for running business for a profit successfully.

There are two sources of ignorance in the school of business: self-ignorance and advisor's ignorance. The worst ignorance a business person safe guide the initial capital against not to sustain a lost is summarily a knowledge gap (self-ignorance) which is when he refused to know what he ought to know.

Knowledge is a kind of leverage in business. Leverage is the ability to do more with little or no money. When we sharpen knowledge, we use less power to cut down a tree with axe.

A bow and arrow do more with less power over a spear; knowledge is a key to wealth procreation.

Knowledge is leverage. Read books that are written by people in the same vision you pursue. Books are also the right places to seek new ideas and knowledge.

A knowledge base investor makes many turnovers with less risk and less working capital. Be knowledgeable and use the mind wisely. Our knowledge is our lever.

We take every battle to the right battlefield in businesses through reading and soul-searching.

The basic three things to invest to grow big money in business are time, knowledge and small money. Do not despise knowledge. Wealth answers to knowledge.

Most people do not invest their time to learn all they supposed to know in business. They lose their money to those who have it. Capital is not as important as knowledge in the school of financial literacy.

We can invest without much money. We can re-invest other People's experience by learning from them.

The desire to learn should drive us than being crazy about money. Some people are not concern about learning except inner crazy fight that is only going on in mind for money. They may end up without even having it.

Learning every day should be our priority.

Every field requires the most learning, experience, education, and skills needed.

To get us out of the reading stress now, we need more fun. One of the most effective ways to learn is by reading and catching fun. It is learning and teaching code.

We do not teach a masquerade how to dance in the public square. He learned before he enters Public Square so that he can always change its dance to the tunes of the instrumentalists by itself without missing. With my teaching so far, I am sure you can dance with the instrumentalist without missing your legs in business. Stay connected.

'You can use small money

to start a small business

but you need broad knowledge

to do business and make

        big MONEY'.

CHAPTER TEN

HANDLE YOUR DEFINING MOMENT

I learned how to control my emotion, and thoughts at a define moment. When emotions are high, focus and responses are tempered with and affected adversely.

People do not take decision when angry. This does not help to affect situation positively, to think well, and take charge of the situation.

The time we are stuck is a define moment. This is also the time when a person has less or no opportunity at all in pursuit of a dream.

Every person had a moment in life that defined a stage when he has failed or faced hindrances, and with little or no achievement.

This is a point in life in which the essential nature or character of a person is revealed and identified. Define moment is a milestone/event which determines all subsequently related occurrences.

We have all had defining moments that have changed our thinking and dispositions.

I once had a define moment, but I thank God for His grace I saw day after day. Thank you God not only for all the blessings but for the frustrations which have helped me become a better person even though I was not born in an affluent home.

My define moments gave me the opportunity to learn better than my peers. Some of the people we faced the same problem are no more while some may be in the drinking bars now. We thank God for His mercy and Grace.

In life, vision is up to us; we do and give what it takes to make it a reality. It takes a long time to become the kind of person we may want to be. We are responsible for what becomes of us no matter how we view it.

Our background, traditions, circumstances may temporally influence whom we are, but they cannot stop us from being the kind of good person we chose to be.

Have a winning spirit. Have a timeless passion that drives performance excellence. This book is an excellent book for a person with the desire to always win, win and win at every defining moments.

'I had engaged in strenuous plowing work

at my define moment ; but it gave me

the opportunity to learn better above my peers'

CHAPTER ELEVEN

WHAT IT TAKES TO BE GREAT:

(1).

(a) Fear of God and Instinct (b) Timing and acting

(d) mentoring

To be great means to be a kind of person in service with right *instinct and acting* in fear of God.

Greatness is when a person has a sense of humor and is exceptional in a given endeavor.

Someone must have right Instinct to be great in his endeavor. Instincts make us flexible and refuse to fix to a pattern.

Timing is also necessary to live a victorious life, and great!

Timing is when watching and acting as at when due. This makes great.

A person (mentor) can help us dream successfully to become great. Find a friend (mentor) who think like you and befriend him in pursuit of that vision of yours.

Many visionaries are stranded because they do not somebody as a mentor.

I often meet my mentor through reading. Someone can contact the spirit of the books he reads. In most cases, I get the best from my mentor(s) in their books. This is one of the reasons whenever my mentor wrote a new book, I quickly buy it because this enables me to upgrade myself.

There is ever a new thing to learn in every new book. I do not often go to my mentor one on one. Very tight and technical problems on how great people have overcome are most shared in books. This is how I get the best from my mentor.

Any time I am stranded, I went on my knee and pray, and also read the books about similar problem, and the answer comes. I read the Bible (the most viable book of management and mentoring in the world).

We have a lot of educated and uneducated people without mentors. They have not acquired skills and nobody has groomed them. The few ones that are groomed are successful and doing well because they were guided (mentored).

Life introduces us to many different people. Some we will love and some we may wish we have never met, but we can learn something different from them.

Have a mentor.

Who is a mentor?

A mentor is that person who will have us do what we do not have what it takes to do on our own, and even when our limitation is causing us to fall, he lifts us.

Our mentor always cares back. This is a person we have in life, not necessarily for money sake. It is far better to have somebody than to have money without having a person.

I am telling us who our mentor is. All the way forward from the cave, people learned their craft by being apprentices to others who guide them, teach them and remold their ideas for them.

Jacob did with his uncle; and Jesus did to John the Baptist. Jesus said to him; I must wash your feet first. To be mentored can also be taken to mean being a servant to someone superior to us over a period to learn.

The purpose of mentoring is to educate, enlighten, and empowered others in an endeavor/ career.

Look for a person who has succeeded on the new road you are about taking. No one claims expertise on a new road without getting crash. This is the reason a role model inform of a mentor should guide us to success.

The reason this topic is inclusive here is that many who had failed were those that were blind in their career. They did not know they do not know it all. 'A person who does not know and yet harden to learn is a fool'.

CHAPTER TWELVE

DO AWAY WITH DARKNESS (CORRUPTION/EVIL):

Darkness is anything that limits and beclouds someone's access to God and progress. Anything that is not permitted by God which we do is called darkness.

Darkness is also anything that beclouds someone's glory. Darkness is someone's limitations and barriers. Darkness is shortcoming.

The instance of darkness is corruption. When a person does not know the difference between wickedness and righteousness, good and bad, it is darkness.

When a person is beclouded with limitations, he lives in darkness. A continuous sinner that lives corrupt life without a reverse of such order is said to be living in darkness.

Living darkness free life is possible. "Is there anything too hard for God? "I am the Lord; the God of all mankind (Jeremiah. 32:27). God desire for us is to stay clear from darkness or all unrighteousness. He takes the darkness away. He turns the ugly situation into the fine situation; He turns every weakness to opportunity, every <u>setback</u> and <u>struggles</u> to <u>blessing</u> and <u>thrives</u>. "Is there anything too hard for God?" (Jer. 32:27). It is not hard for God to take away darkness from us.

Friends!

Tough times never last. No matter how tough is that situation or cloud that beclouds us; the mercy of God prevails. His love and mercy never come to an end, and it doesn't say, goodbye.

Faith and the right attitude can keep us when darkness traces us that the courage to stand against that which beclouds us has failed.

Darkness is chaff; grain becomes more useful at the time the chaffs are removed from them. Darkness is anything that can hide our beauty; chaff does that.

A person may have enough food to eat, a fleet of cars to drive and many houses to live in; but this does not mean that the person is out of darkness and living crises free life. Life without fear of God is full of darkness or chaffs.

That sin which has refused to take a leave is darkness: lies, adultery, fornication, stealing, idle talk, bad-mouthing, drunkenness, fake manifestoes, racism, fake promises, usury, they are all dark and lusts of this world.

A man is enslaved by what he cannot overcome, just like sin.

As we may all know, chaffs are separated from the grains because it dirties the wheat.

God's love is guaranteed. He takes darkness away

from us (Psalm. 107:14).

CHAPTER THIRTEEN

A ZERO BASE SUCCESS

Man is a light that needs three component things to shine and retain its fullness. This component thing is right attitude; self-control and the fear of God.

Those things add value to life in fullness and make us overcome darkness and behave well.

Man's relationship with people is in correlation with his relationship with God. Whether it is power or knowledge we have, it is of no value when it cannot fix a problem, and save others or impacts.

Life is about donation. Success is not in the accumulation of wealth measures in the hands and bank account without lifting others with it; but a fulfilment arose on impacting others to actualize.

Success and greatness is not necessarily the much that is bequeathed to children except when what is bequeathed is properly harnessed then it makes great!

Inheritance without a dream is a waste.

Many people are looting, doing evil to be rich and famous all for a reason their children should not suffer the way they did and not to live below poverty level. No! This is not a legacy.

Who said the children would not suffer the consequences of this evil deed, or subsequently be poorer and hunger-stricken? Do we know excess wind fall can make us learn only consumption behavior which leads to poverty?

When children see their parents as spend thrifts, they learn from them. Looted money is not valued and it's spent carelessly. It is the worst ever spent. Stolen waters quench thirst but the worst ever drank, food eaten in secret is delicious but it cause stomach disorder. Thus is the behavior of stolen money.

Nobody has ever stolen and still claim to be trusted, great and better than others without being condemned.

But who is greater (Luke. 22:25- 27) as it is written..., "he who sits at the table or he who serves? Is it not he who sits at the table? I am among you as the one who serves".

Here, Jesus redefined the meaning of greatness and reversed the values, principles, standards, ethics, and idea of the world about greatness to be measured in the line of good service, not even a thought of idleness and unearned riches – corruption.

The background of one's parents does not count in pursuing success; it is by predestination everyone is born into a particular family. One cannot choose a biological father while as we have the freedom to choose a spiritual pathway that will make us great!

Our future sees beyond where we are coming from. We ought to start at a very humble beginning to a greater height and allow God to take the front seat of our drives.

We do not allow the one penny of today to snatch our big future. Looted wealth is the worst ever spent by man. Let our children learn, let them work, and be free from violence and tell them free things are most times, not precious things.

Anything that has value has a price, pay it to get it. Teach children the proper use of money, so they do not grow up becoming spend thrifts. Tell them to relate well with their families and others.

*Let them learn to work and earn money from jobs/ self-developments, serve God with it and give to the nee*dy. Teach them not to allow money to become the lord of their lives. We must rescue our generation from this nonsense.

Let me point to some personalities, some of our forefathers: Isaac, Abraham, Jacob, Elisha etc).

Isaac did not only lived on his father's (Abraham) wealth but he also planted and harvested a hundred fold in a single year on the land he inherited from his father.

Jacob did not depend on the wealth of his father Isaac, but he was sustained on the covenant platform of working hard for his blessings.

He sent his children to Egypt with money to buy grain during that age far economic meltdown, the period when the power of money failed in the land.

Jacob's water well in Samaria has today become a reference in the Bible (John. 4:6) at where Jesus met the Samaritan woman for waters.

Elisha was from a wealthy home, his father had twelve yokes of oxen engaged in plowing, yet he did not allow his son to grow up grasping. It was while Elisha was usefully engaged in the performance of his duty, *undertaking the strenuous work of plowing that he received a divine call.* Elisha was a farmer who lived with his parents (1 king. 19:16-21). He maintained his own house in Samaria (2kings. 6:32)

David was sent for in the bush as a nomadic to lead is people; these are few riddles with meaning so teach you and your children the proper way to live a life.

We all know that poverty (deficiency in resources) is not good. In the first place, there is nothing wrong with men possessing wealth. A good man leave inheritance for his children's children; but the wrong comes in when wealth possesses their owners.

Wealth of sinners is laid up for the just (Proverbs. 13:12).

Proverbs 10:15 also demonstrated that the rich man wealth is his strong city (strength). It is a good thing to be wealthy, but the wrong comes when riches ruin men.

Train a child in the way he should go, and when he is old, he will not depart from it (Proverbs.

22: 6). We profane our children's destinies by making them mere spend thrifts. Tell them money earned is better than a gift and to steal.

The venom of a viper does no harm a tortoise. Work does not kill.

Make good use of your time and weaknesses and stop doing the wrong things. We need money because it gives us a voice. Let's put our hands and knowledge at work together to earn us some money. Teach our children love, how to work and a peaceful way to follow one another.

Are our children prepared to inherit us ? It is the well trained children that will take the inheritance as in the instance of the following story:

The only son of a certain wealthy man was to inherit the father's wealth/businesses when he shall die. The elder gave him one condition to be met: Go and earn ten thousand dollars and bring it to me. My multi-million dollars business will be handed over to you when I die. "You shall manage my businesses", the old man added.

In no long time, his son brought him the money he had collected from his mother, claiming he worked for it. Though his father welcomed him and collected the money from him, and threw it inside his burning oven. The two watched the oven until the money was burnt to ashes.

The old man told his son to go and work for fifteen Thousand dollars and bring it to him. After many weeks, he came back to the father with the money. His mother had given him the money again and told the boy to wait for some times without eating food so he could look disguised in the sight of his father. He did as he was instructed by his mother.

When he met his father with the money, he took the cash (fifteen thousand dollars) from him and threw it into the burner, and they watched the fifteen Thousand dollars burnt to ashes.

Then he told his son to go and work to earn Five Thousand Dollars this time and bring it to him again.

The boy went and met his mother for advice. Many options were fashioned out to raise this money by the mother to outsmart the old man; but at last, the boy decided to go and earn the Five Thousand dollars and give it to his father. He refused her mother's advice at this time.

The boy now traveled to another town where he did hard plowing and menial jobs to get the money. He went very far to places nobody knew him as a child of a wealthy man.

He at this time worked for the money. He spent months denied himself unnecessary spending and pleasures of the flesh and stopped all sort of luxury life accustomed to some children born and raised in a bad rich Family just to save the Five thousand dollars.

When he finally came home, his mother could not recognize her son. She burst into tears and murmured "What a wicked Father!" but the boy was excited for solely working and saving Five Thousand dollars by himself to give to his Father.

With that desperate condition, he quickly went and presented the money to his father who was again incidentally using the burner/oven.

He gave his father the money, and again he threw it inside the burning oven; but the boy shouted, "Daddy!" and dived to the oven and brought the cashout and exclaimed: Daddy! Don't burn it! The father asked him, "why should I not burn this one"?

The son answered and said: we do not waste money. We do not allow our sweat to be lavished and carelessly. The father then said: you have worked for this money my son. Nobody will stand looking, watching his effort being burnt, wasted as we had done in the previous ones. It was your mother that gave you the money before.

Friends! Inheritance without a dream is a waste.

Train yourself and your family on the proper way to use money so that they do not grow up to be looters and only spend thrifts. Many Looters and spend thrifts hardly know how to manage money in the Economy. They print more money into the circulation when it got finished, and they melt down the economy.

The truth is that the economic power of one's parents can influence his/ her child's ascendancy and put him or her on a right direction to go in life.

When such economic power and intellect are well utilized on a child, his or her future as well as the society will be safe.

Why do we engage in corruption that kills? Someone does not have to steal /kill to be great. We need God and people to live, do your best to stop indulging in corruption and indecent lifestyle.

What is refer to a zero base success is the rising from nothing to something in grace and truth without covetousness or stealing. I believe we will choose to have this success.

We do not allow our background to put our back to the ground or poison our future with the pain of the past due to poor background that ruptures dreams and success.

God never consults our past to determine our future. A man may be needy now, poor or sick in the body and yet a friend of God marked for success to impact. We have a cause to live. A person who has a cause to champion bears and understands that venom does tortoise no harm. We work into greatness with understanding and by working hard to the right direction.

Success is always hard to attain and makes someone feel like quitting. If we want to reach the peak, we must cherish small beginning, humble ourselves, and we will experience Fulfilment.

We do not become great to start; we start very small and become very great. When a Person thinks too big to start with a little, he may also be too big and heavy for a lifting by God. Small opportunities are often the beginning of greater enterprise.

Success is actualization on the sacrifice we made to overcome oppositions we encountered, the struggles against overwhelming odds and the courage with which we have maintained focus.

Someone can achieve success effortlessly even while in the valley. A person in a valley looks up for a lifting; not down.

Difficulties are builders. There has never been somebody who has never had a defining moment so love challenges because this encourages us to do more.

A person without a problem is a dead man. A challenge is a twig to higher height. The sky should be your starting point, not even your limit.

'A challenge is a resistant that says to us; we would n't get there when we are going.' A resistant always wants to displace us and give us a near breakthrough. Those resistances may include: fear, ignorance, We cannot, I can't, self-deception, people will say, and what people would say, poverty, I have not known much; but know that you will never know it all or have all you need to start, start working to show the little you have known. You can start it now.

Success is like a case won. A case won is a problem put to rest and every problem solved becomes a case study/ reference. Our success can be a reference from which others learn.

folded hands fails and have no glory for not fulfilling a course. Wake up! I am not speaking against wealth but when craving for idle hands wealth which result into corruption.

"Money is a defense" (Ecclesiastes.7:12). The love of it makes one go wrong. We do not have to earn a bad name and demean our selves because of money.

We do not have to travel afar before we become the kind of person we chose to be. The fortunes we are looking outside for is in us. We have over one billion mineral deposits inside us undermined. With this, we can defeat others drive.

Avoid "I must travel out of my country" mentality. This desperate desire has destroyed many destiny. Some people once traveled and missed their opportunities while some could not get back home.

Perhaps, I do not see traveling to far places for fortune as the only solution or end to a struggle or lack. Some people often think that their destiny is in a specific place. There is no poor land anywhere; there is no poor brain anywhere. All land and brain are blessed use it.

All Adam needed in the Garden of Eden to be happy was inside him unknown. *Eve was inside Adam unknown to him until she was formed out of him.* All we need to achieve in life are inside us at where we are unknown.

I can see the gold you are looking for inside you (a very titanic idea is in you unknown, it is creativity). Are you following me? **Tire Ni O!** (All is yours o!).

This believe (I must relocate without seeking God's opinion) can destroy a great plan and idea. Our destiny is inside us, It is located anywhere we are. There is nothing in a far country if we are not led by God comparable with what God has for us at where we are. We can make where we are today sightseeing. We should emancipate ourselves from slavery. None but our God and minds can free us

Russia President, Vladimir Putin as he has rightly said, "Africa is a cemetery for Africans. When an African becomes rich, his bank accounts are in Switzerland. He travels to France for medical treatment.

He invests in Germany. He buys from Dubai. He consumes Chinese. He prays in Rome, or Mecca. His children study in Europe. He travels to Canada, USA, and Europe for tourism.

If he dies, he will be buried in his native country of Africa. Africa is just a cemetery for Africans. How could a cemetery be developed?"

Hold on to what is around you and the opportunities you have. Where we are is not the problem but what we do with it in this century of global connections for rapid development.

Do you know opportunity may lie within the smallest undiscovered opportunity around you? Do what you can with what you have at where you are and you will have a good success. May God open our eyes.

The way we think may also be one of the reasons we may find no end, meaning that we are our minds which makes and bring us what we want.

Our destiny is control by two forces, *you and God.* If we succeed, it is God and we; but when we have failed, we are held responsible because God does not fail.

Are you currently the unsuccessful among the successful? Is it so? Good! Listen to this: behind every successful man there is a lot of unsuccessful years. A successful man was an unachieved person. That you may not have succeeded does not mean you are a failure. One day is one day. Just keep trying.

Pray to God .When we pray God comes in.

Friends!

If we see a person or a nation that is greater than we are, we fine out what is it they do we do not do. May God give us better understanding.

Success is also in knowing something nobody else knows which we know, then we do it.

Let every man has an appointment with himself and with God. Winners always see the strength of God in battles.

Some people also believe that they can only be lifted by bringing someone else down. Stop pulling people down. That is witchcraft hurting. Stop fighting others. That is not the ground rule to succeed in life.

Do you know a person that loves and kind is joyful and feels fulfilled because he is doing the Lord's will? He may not be fulfilled even when he is given a house or a car or a place of prominence- vanity.

Don't go wrong because of position or money (the third principal actor of this world). Remember that vanity of vanities, says the preacher; all is vanity (Ecclesiastes. 12: 8).

Start from a zero base and know that sudden success and working outside God's will is none sense. We can say no to corruption when we realize that with God's grace we can do all things and be more than conquerors.

What house are we going to build in exchange for the soul that is so precious? If our pleasures are not in godliness, forget it.

Comment: In the above chapter the entire mood of the author is aligned. The preacher has not found and seen anything of lasting value in man's life outside salvation. Then why should a man choose evil because of worldly things since life itself is vanity?

What house can someone build just for pleasure in exchange for his soul? If our treasures are not in line with God's plan for us, forget it(Isaac Jacob)

'Perhaps, I do not think to travel to far places is the solution or an end to a struggle or lack.

Some people thought their destiny is

in a specific place. It might be closer than they may think.

What Adam needed to be happy was inside him unknown.

Eve was in Adam's body unknown to him until she was formed out of him.

All we need to be achieved and to experience fulfiment in our endeavor is inside us. We extract it. 'Stop going everywhere'

CHAPTER FOURTEEN

THE VERY TITANIC STORY-YOU WILL LEARN

An impoverished newly wedded young couple lived in a small tent where he farm. One day he made the following proposal to his wife.

Honey! I will leave the house and travel far away to get a job that will give us the comfortable life that we deserve. I do not know how long I will stay away. You should be faithful to me, and I will be faithful to you. So the young man left. He lost communication with the wife all through.

He walked many days until he found a rich farmer who was in need of someone to help him. The young man introduced his service to the farmer, and he was accepted for the work. Therefore, he discussed the terms with the Boss:

Let me work for as long as I wanted, and when I t think I should go home, please release me of my duties. I do not want to receive my salary. Save it for me until the day I leave which is the day I decided to go. Please give me the money, and I will go my way.

They agreed on that; so the young man worked for twenty-two years faithfully without rest. When it was the last day of the years, he came to his boss and said:

Boss, I want my money because I am returning to my home.

The boss replied:

All right, after all, I made a deal with you, and I will stick to it. However, before you go, I want to give you something, not salaries:

"I will give you all your money and send you away, or I will give you three pieces of advice and send you away. If I give you the money, I will not give you the three pieces of advice. And if I give you the three pieces of advice, I will not give the money. Now go to the lodge and think about that for a choice.

He thought for three days. Then he went to the boss and told him:

I want the three pieces of advice, and the boss stressed it again, I will not give you the money

And the man replied:

I want the three pieces of advice. The boss then told him:

(1).Never takes shortcuts in life. Shorter and unknown path can cost someone life.

(2).Never be too curious for curiosity can be deadly

(3).Never decides in a moment of anger or pains because when you repent, it could be too late.

After given him the three pieces of advice, the boss said to him: here are three loaves of bread.

Two are for you to eat on your journey and the last is for you to eat with your wife when you get home.

So the man went his way after twenty-two years away from home and from his wife whom he loved so much.

After the first day of the travel, he found a man who welcomed him, a sympathizer and asked: "where are you going?"

He replied: To a distant place "Uwano" which is about twenty days away if I continue walking.

The man shouted and said to him: O!, this path is too long! I know a shortcut that is very safe, and you will arrive in less than five days.

The man began to follow the path suggested to him until he remembered the first piece of advice. Then he returned and followed the long path.

Three days later, he learned that the shortcut leads to an ambush. After another three days of the journey, he found an inn by the roadside, where he could rest. He paid for a room, and after taking a bath, he lay down and slept off.

During the night he woke up as he heard a terrifying scream. It was not a dream. He rose to his feet and went to the door; he remembers the second piece of advice. Therefore he returned to his bed. In the morning after breakfast, the owner of the lodging asked him, if he had not heard the scream at night. He affirmed that he heard.

Then the host said- were you not curious to see what happened?

And he replied,

No, I was not.

Then the host said:

You are the first to leave this guest in and live. My neighbor is completely crazy. He usually shouts at night to call someone's attention. When some of the guests come out, he killed them and buried their bodies in the backyard after taken their blood. Is the host different from his neighbor, I ask?

The man continues his long journey eager to arrive soon.

After many days and nights walking, he was exasperated, but he finally saw his house far away. It was the night. He saw some light coming out of the window of his house and was able to see his wife. She was not alone.

When he saw that scene, his heart was filled with hatred and bitterness. He decided to rush and kill them both mercilessly.

However, he remembered the third piece of advice. Then he stopped, reflected and decided to sleep outside that night. He slept in the midst of the bushes around his tent, determined to make a decision the next day.

At dawn, he was calmer and thought:

I will not kill my wife and her love. I am going back to my boss to ask him to take me back. However, before I go, I will not rush into this decision. I want to tell my wife that I have always been faithful to her.

He went to the front door and knocked when his wife opened the door and saw him; she cried and embraced him warmly. He tried to push her away, *but he was not able. Then with tears in his eyes, he said to her: I was faithful to you, but you betrayed me.*

She was shocked. So she replied:

How did I betray you? I have never betrayed you. I waited patiently for you for twenty-two good years. Then he said:

How about the man that you were caressing yesterday?

She said:

That man is your son. When you left, I discovered I was pregnant. Today he is twenty-two years old.

Hearing that, the man asked her forgiveness. He went and hugged his son.

Then he told them all the things he had experienced while away. His wife prepared some meal for them to eat together.

After, the last bread given by his boss after a prayer of thanksgiving was broken. When he looked at it, he found all his money inside. There was even more than the right payment for his twenty-two years of dedication, faithfulness, and hard work.

Our God is like this Boss, and you are like that faithful servant. When He speaks to us, tells us what not to do, he wants to give us a right end; more than what we give Him. He wants us to have life, as well as the material blessings to prove that He dwells among us.

OTHER BOOKS WRITTEN BY DISCIPLE ERAGA E JACOB

-The Bowl of Treasures (An Insight to Light)

-Fame to Fulfilment: The Secrets to Achieving Fulfilment.

-Addressing the Societal Problem: Corruption, & Creating Values in Africa.

-The Wonder of Grace.

THE AUTHOR:

A Person You Should Know: Apostle Evangelist. Eraga E. Jacob

- Don't look back when you should not. Don't stress over things that don't matters. Don't worry about things you cannot manage.

- God will wreck your plans when He sees that your plans will wreck you

Apostle Eraga E Jacob is a man of Grace; plain, and has insight to the revealed truth. He strongly believes in God, and that all puzzles of life answer to God in mystery.

He swaps the world with his <u>stringent anti-Corruption crusade Movement</u> through the preaching of the message (Word) of Grace and truth (John .1: 17); walking against ungodliness for salvation (unspotted life).

In undertaking this phase of the divine order, the Apostle uses different medium which includes hand bills, audio CD, tapes, books, elocutions for his out-reach changing the world.

Apostle (Evan) Eraga E .Jacob hobbies are: Reading, Running, Reasoning and Writing (RRRW).He has written several books on different endeavors impacting lives. He hates excuses, what only sees the reasons we cannot proceed, and he sees discouragement as the courage to work harder. He is also a synonym of faith, kindness, and he rules his **word.**

Eraga E. Jacob is a minister, a teacher and a resourceful entrepreneur. His registered trade mark is AIJ.

Mrs. Eraga Faith Lawrenta is his wife. Their marriage is blessed with children: Abraham, Isaac & Jacob Junior. They love almost as much as he does

www.ingramcontent.com/pod-product-compliance
Lightning Source LLC
Chambersburg PA
CBHW021406210526
45463CB00001B/239